# YOUR VOICE

SINGING SIMPLIFIED FOR EVERY SINGER

## SUPPORT

## SHAPE

## CONTROL

BY IVETA SHVED-TANG

*Your Voice*
Singing Simplified For Every Singer, Support Shape Control
by Iveta Shved-Tang
Copyright © 2020

Distributed by:
Harmon-ee Music
Singapore, 733571
UEN: 53396535K
harmon-ee-music.business.site

ISBN: 978-981-14-6580-2 (softcover revised)

Back cover photo: Jovan Tang
Interior photo: Marta April Photography



Published in Singapore

*I would like to dedicate this book to my first mentor, Olga Pougatch. Thank you for seeing something in me and taking me under your wing when I was only 15 years old. So much of where I am today started with you and continues to flourish. This book is one of the many fruits produced from all those years you've invested in me.*

*Thank you for never giving up on me.*

*I love you so much!*

# CONTENTS

# ENDORSEMENTS

*"A comprehensive overview of the fundamentals of singing, Iveta has captured the holistic perspective of a teacher, performer and recording artist. This book intimately showcases the authenticity of her music with practical tips from her performing experiences."*

**Aldrich Atcoustic**
Singer/Songwriter & Recording Artist
Founder of Atcoustic Live Music
**Singapore**

*"It takes very little to see Iveta's passion and gifting for the voice. I have had the honour of offering Iveta's instruction to students at our music and recording school, in both one on one settings as well as workshops/camps. I know first hand how rare it is to find a vocal instructor that is not only knowledgeable and articulate, but able to work with a wide array of vocal abilities and challenges. The students at our studio have benefited immensely from Iveta's coaching, as I have personally heard incredible improvement across the board. However, the best indication of a great instructor is having students share how thrilled they have been with their progression while showing a newfound confidence in their skills."*

**Aubrey Bouskill**
Singer/Songwriter & Recording Artist
Owner of Harmony Studios
**Anaheim, California**

*"As a producer it's always a pleasure to work with talented artists and musicians who master their craft. Working with Iveta on her album, 'Only One,' was a windows view of her passion for music, songwriting and vocal performance. Her technique both in and out of the studio are exemplary. She never sacrifices her strive for vocal perfection and maintains an honest representation of exactly what is needed for the song to come to life."*

**Erwin Rocha**
Singer/Songwriter & Recording Artist
Owner/Producer of Redi Records
**Anaheim, California**

# TESTIMONIALS

*"Iveta is a fantastic and experienced vocal teacher. She has helped me to refine my vocal techniques. In the past, I constantly struggled to maintain my voice after singing, but after learning from Iveta I have grown to skilfully project my voice without difficulty. Iveta is passionate about unlocking your potential, and truly believes that structured training and encouragement will bring out the best in your vocal journey."*

**Cheng Jun Wong**
Account Manager
Healthcare Logistics
**Singapore**

*"I always loved music growing up, but I never had the confidence to sing for anyone other than my family. I met Iveta at a church I attended in college where we both served as part of the worship band. I asked Iveta to teach me everything about singing and music. Iveta was a wonderful teacher! She taught me music theory and proper vocal technique. She identified my weaknesses and helped me develop exercises to improve them. I can truly say that I am a more confident vocalist because of Iveta. I will forever be grateful to her!"*

**Michelle Kalu**
Doctor of Pharmacy
PhD Graduate Student
**Los Angeles, California**

"Iveta is a great teacher! I'm so thankful for her very loving, patient and generous approach to teaching. I was able to improve my singing in every lesson such as how to expand my vocal range and project my voice. I am amazed by her beautiful voice and enjoyed hearing about her life experiences during our time together."

**Abby Hee**
Account Manager
Information Technology
**Penang, Malaysia**

# ACKNOWLEDGMENTS

*Thank you to my vocal coach, Larisa Bryski. I will always cherish our sessions together working on original music. You've played a major part in my singing journey. Thank you for instilling the skill and confidence in me to sing!*

*Thank you to my husband and partner, Jovan Tang. I could not have done this without your love, support and constant encouragement. You truly are a gift from God! Life with you is the most amazing adventure, and I look forward to the many more wonderful endeavours ahead of us!*

*Thank you to my parents, Sergey and Evia Shved.*
*You've been there through every major transition in my life. Thank you for putting me through all those piano and vocal lessons over the years, and for your constant support and encouragement towards the call of God over my life. I love and honour you.*

*Thank you to Shirley Bridwell. You are continually an inspiration to me and Jovan. You have taught us so much on how to steward the gift of God in us and to use it for His purpose and glory!*
*Thank you for loving and supporting us the way that you do!*
*Love you so very much!*

*Thank you to Erwin and Aubrey for taking a chance with me by taking me on to teach and record at Harmony Studios. You both are an answered prayer! You not only have taught me and supported my music, but have walked with me through my ups and downs. I am so grateful to God for giving me an amazing big brother and sister! I know that God has many more great things in store for you and your family! Love you both!*

# INTRODUCTION

To better understand your voice, I'd like to break it down into three individual elements: support, shape and control. In order for our voices to function efficiently and to maintain good stamina, it's important to understand and strengthen every element.

If we cannot maintain our intake of air and balance our air flow, or correctly shape our mouths to influence our tone, volume and diction, the ability to control our voices will decrease, which will contribute to vocal strain and pitch issues.

Regardless of the genre or style of music you are looking to sing in, having a strong support system, accurate shape and good control, will give you the longevity and ability you need for crafting and developing your sound.

My hope is that when you read this book, your understanding to singing would be simplified and made practical. Because you are the instrument, teaching your body how to produce the sound you want takes patience and appropriate amounts of exercise. Taking professional vocal lessons in addition to reading this book is highly recommended. May this book help you get started in becoming the singer you both desire and are meant to be!

The following chapters will be discussed in the form of most commonly asked questions.

# CHAPTER ONE
## SUPPORT

### *What is the support system?*

Our support system is our respiratory system. Let's start with the diaphragm. The diaphragm is a muscle beneath your lungs, or at the lowest part of your ribcage. In order for your lungs to maintain enough air, the diaphragm will contract and move downwards as you inhale. When you exhale, the diaphragm will move upwards, back into its original position. Try taking a deep breath through the nose for three seconds, and exhale out of the mouth slowly with an "oo" shape. See how your belly pops out? That's your diaphragm moving downwards!

To further understand this phenomenon, let's imagine a tube of toothpaste. Have you ever seen the tool that helps you squeeze the toothpaste out? Imagine that tool is your diaphragm and the toothpaste is your air. Whenever you start to run out of toothpaste, the tool will push upwards to squeeze the remaining toothpaste out. The same thing happens with your lungs. As you use air to sing, the diaphragm pushes the air in your lungs upwards and out until your next breath.

### *How can a strong diaphragm help me sing better?*

Developing a strong support system will give you the capability to hold out your notes longer as well as help you control your singing technique. You will be able to stabilise your notes more effectively without the shakiness! Try taking a solid breath and sing out a comfortable note using, "ahh." Have a little fun with it and time yourself to see how long you can hold it out. Make sure you are feeling your diaphragm engaged as it's slowly moving upwards, supporting the air. You will notice as you run out of air, the less control you'll have of your singing, and the tighter the squeeze will be in your abdomen. Therefore, remember to take good breaths!

### How do I strengthen the diaphragm?

We can strengthen the diaphragm with various exercises. Let's start with the *balloon exercise* as I'd like to call it. Make sure you are maintaining good posture for this with your back straight. You may sit, stand or lie down on your back. Take in a deep breath through the nose and imagine your diaphragm moving downwards as you inhale. Like the opening of a balloon, allow a very small amount of air to pass through your mouth while making a *"sss"* sound. You may even consider timing yourself as well to test your lung capacity. Thirty seconds or more is considered a good time.

You can also practice deep breathing to strengthen your diaphragm. Again, you can choose to sit, stand or lie down on your back. If you choose to lie down, try placing something like a book on top of your stomach. As you breathe, you should be able to see the book move up and down. You can visualise the toothpaste example for greater efficiency. Even regularly blowing up balloons can strengthen your lung capacity and diaphragm over time.

Remember that while singing, you'll need to engage the diaphragm especially when you're projecting your voice, holding out notes for long periods of time, and when you are singing in your upper range.

### I'm taking a good breath, but I still seem to be running out of air.

If you are experiencing loss of air quickly, even though you took a pretty good breath, the issue lies in either your shape or your vocal control, which I will expound on in chapters two and three. The idea is maintain a balanced flow of air while singing. It's best to avoid any forced pushes of air coming from your throat.

*Tip:*

If the back of your throat is too open, the air will spread out, which will cause you to run out of air much faster. Very often I've noticed singers who have this issue add an "h" sound before the word they are singing. Words using an "h," naturally produce a breathier sound. Try to avoid any unnecessary "h" sounds while singing. If you are singing a word such as, "heart," try emphasising the latter part of the word more by keeping the "h" sound soft and without over singing it.

# CHAPTER TWO
## SHAPE

Shape in other words, is your mouth. Your mouth mainly influences three elements: tone, volume and diction. Let's take a closer look at each element.

### Tone

Your tone can also be categorised as timbre, or the quality of sound your voice can produce. The lower your larynx, or voice box, the warmer and fuller your sound becomes. The higher you raise your larynx, the brighter and thinner your tone will become. For example, classical and theatre music use a lowered larynx in much of their singing technique as compared to other styles of music. To better illustrate, try singing any note while yawning. This sensation will naturally lower your larynx and produce a warmer tone. You can also try raising your larynx by singing the word, "tea," which produces a brighter tone. Did you notice the tightness in your jaw? This will naturally raise your larynx up, as "tea" uses consonants. Consonants pronounced correctly are shaped with a smile, which are speech sounds other than vowels (a, e, i, o, u).

### Volume

It may sound obvious, but opening your mouth well enough while you sing or speak, will help you increase in volume and vocal presence. We can also categorise volume as dynamics. It's important to use a variety of dynamics in your singing to elevate your performance. To project your sound, make sure you have taken a good breath while maintaining proper *vocal placement,* (see chapter three). As you sing out your first note, remember you should feel your abdomen engaged. You can also imagine you are trying to get a person's attention who is at the opposite side of the room. To make sure your mouth is open enough, try the two finger rule by measuring the opening of your mouth with the width of your middle and index fingers together.

## Diction

Diction is how you enunciate or pronounce your words. Depending on what language you are singing in will determine the way your mouth will be shaped. When speaking or singing, pronouncing your words correctly is important so that you are able to communicate clearly. Singing will require you to sometimes stretch out words longer than if you were to speak them. To do this correctly, let's begin with the word, "no." "No" is made up of one consonant and two vowel sounds (n, o and oo).

Let's sing and stretch out the word, "no," for three seconds. For clarity, the letter you should be holding out the longest is "o." The first and last sounds should normally not be stretched out for very long. I find this keeps the word easy to understand while singing. Remember to stay true to the natural shape of the mouth. If you are stretching out "o," then remember to only change to the "oo" shape at the very end. You can practice your vowel and consonant sounds while warming up using: mama, yaya, no and ee.

As mentioned previously, consonants will naturally raise your larynx and tighten your law. While this can brighten up your tone, it can also effect your vocal control and cause your voice to strain. It's best to keep your larynx in a neutral position as much as possible for a balanced sound. Vowels, on the other hand, are the best for singing because they naturally keep the larynx low and relaxed.

# CHAPTER THREE
## CONTROL

**What is considered good vocal control?**

Vocal control is our vocal placement. Vocal placement is where the voice is resonating. I'd like to think of it as your stirring wheel for singing. In order for us to sing with ease, we must practice good vocal placement, or in other words, singing from the mask of the face. When we engage our facial muscles, we are influencing the resonance of sound to the front of the face. This helps us avoid adding additional pressure on the vocal folds, which will cause vocal strain. This skill takes time and practice in order for it to become natural and consistent.

**I feel that I am straining my voice, especially on the high notes.**

When air passes through your trachea (windpipe), then through your vocal folds, it is called phonation. The idea is to allow the air to move easily from the throat to avoid vocal strain. Vocal strain is when we squeeze the throat muscles while singing or speaking. This will tighten the vocal folds, and result in vocal damage over a period of time. Pushing from the throat will limit the ability to sing with ease. The tightness will also limit the range of notes you can sing as well as the various ways you can texturise your voice. Take a break if you have pain when you sing as you are most likely experiencing inflammation in your voice box. It's best to see a specialist or take some professional vocal lessons for training.

I like using visuals while singing as visuals can help us maintain better vocal control, and achieve different techniques with the voice. Let's imagine you know someone named, "Yaya," who is at the far end of the same room as you. You are looking to get their attention, and unless you raise your voice, you will not be heard.

Try visualising this moment while calling out, "Yaya!" Be careful not to scream, but simply raise your voice enough to be heard. You should feel your diaphragm contract. If done correctly, you won't feel any strain on your vocal folds. "Yaya" is great to use while warming up your voice because of it's natural tendency to pull your jaw down. If not all, most singers have experienced vocal strain because of their lack of air, relaxed shape and correct placement.

Let's try another exercise. I want you to flex your nose muscles as if something smells really bad. At the same time, stretch out the word, "mama." You should feel the resonance in your nose. This exercise will help reset your placement to the face. Try doing the same thing while singing higher notes. You will notice it will be easier to sing the notes without the strain. While I don't encourage nasal singing, this is a good exercise to strengthen forward placement. Overtime, this will feel more natural to you. The next time you sing or warm up your voice, flex your nose muscles throughout. Use a visual such as throwing darts or tossing a football to enforce forward placement.

### What are vocal registers?

Vocal registers can be defined as different modes or vocal timbre your voice produces. Timbre is a colour or quality of sound. It is the different ways your vocal folds vibrate that influence these sounds. To simplify, these registers can be broken up into chest voice, head voice and mix voice. These registers also usually occupy a certain range of notes.

### Chest Voice

Let's start with the chest voice. The chest voice register can be very similar a person's speaking voice. Try placing your hand on your chest as you read or sing in a low to comfortable key. Do you feel your chest vibrate? This means you are in your chest register, as your chest will vibrate. In terms of the sound quality, this register normally will vibrate at lower pitches with a warm and broad timbre.

## Head Voice

Head voice is often called falsetto, which technically defines a male singer in his head voice or upper range. It's called falsetto because this register sounds so different as compared to a man's speaking voice, that it's considered his "false" voice. This register is also known as having an airier texture. Most often, when singing in your head voice, you will feel the resonance of sound in your head. After singing in this register for a while, you may start to feel light headed. To understand this register better, keep your hand on your chest, and sing a high note using, "hee." The tone should sound breathier with less vibrations in your chest. The execution should not feel forced.

## Mix Voice

Mix voice is a combination of both registers, or the "in between" notes. This register includes the notes just before your voice "breaks, " or in other words, changes to the head voice register. Although the resonance begins to shift to your head, you are still using similar muscle function as your chest voice. This register resonates in your nasal cavities, which explains why the tone sounds bright and compressed. If you can recall our discussion earlier regarding vocal placement, singing in the mix register is where singers are most susceptible to vocal strain. The higher the notes you sing, the greater the pressure and tension exist between your vocal folds. This is where maintaining proper vocal placement is especially crucial. Some styles of singing intentionally place a little more pressure on the vocal folds in order to obtain a grittier sound, which include growls and cracks. This can be known as vocal fry and should be done with caution.

### How do low and high notes work?

When singing lower notes, vibrations on the vocal folds are slower with greater volumes of air passing through them. The vocal folds are thicker with less pressure. I find that it's often easier to sing the really low notes when my approach to them is softer and airier, therefore, over projecting them is unnecessary. If you are having trouble maintaining good volume, make sure your mouth is open enough.

Higher notes are just the opposite. The vibrations are faster with less volumes of air passing through the vocal folds. You may think of it as a stretched rubber band. The opening becomes smaller, therefore, creating more pressure and higher pitches. Another register that includes very high notes is called the whistle register. The notes sung in this register can sound like you are squeaking, but given enough practice, you can eventually develop good control and apply them in your performances.

# CHAPTER FOUR

## VOCAL PERFORMANCE

### *What is considered good vocal performance?*

Now that we have discussed how to correctly support, shape and control your singing, managing your vocal performance will become easier and more intentional. Good vocal performance is when you are able to balance all three elements well, while translating the feel and message of your song authentically. The first step is to know your song melodically, rhythmically and lyrically. This will help you build your confidence in the song, and will allow you to focus on how you want translate the song emotionally. I find it's more impactful to move your your audience emotionally in addition to singing technically well. Most people will remember how you made them feel rather than producing a technically perfect performance. It's ok to make mistakes!

### *What are some ways I can express myself while singing?*

A great start would be using body language. Body language can help your audience understand your song better. It's a great way to portray the emotion and message behind the song. Try moving around more than just standing in one place. Use your hands, arms and facial expressions to describe how you feel. Visuals and lyrics are helpful for inspiration. For example, if the lyric says, "I surrender," try extending your arms and hands out while getting on your knees. Some performers will even grab the entire microphone stand with them while they move around the stage!

If a particular section is more meaningful to you, try accenting it by changing up or adding notes (runs), increasing or decreasing the dynamics, changing the tone, adding vibrato, and shortening or lengthening the notes. The idea is to be creative and bring the song to life!

### What is improvising, and how do I apply this to my singing?

Many times, singers will improvise or change up the melody, rhythm or lyrics of a song. This could also mean to add a spontaneous moment to the song. Improvising takes practice and a certain level of confidence in both your vocal control and familiarity with the song. During musical breaks, I will often add or elaborate certain lyrics based off my song using my own melody, according to the key I am in.

### How do I add runs?

You can think of runs as additional notes, normally based off a musical scale, or key. To keep things simple, you can use the scale belonging to the song you are singing. Many popular songs use the major scale. If you are familiar with the solfeggio method, you can try singing this: "do, re, mi, fa, sol, la, ti, do!" For singing runs, use any of these pitches to add additional notes to your song. You can do this by stretching out a particular lyric, or adding a vowel sound by using 1-2 extra notes. You can also change the speed of the run depending on the time signature, or rhythm of the song. Practice improvising by doing a little at a time. Find a favourite section of the song and start from there. Runs are often added at the end of melodic phrases. I find that listening and observing other singers helps me get inspired to find my own way of using runs!

### How do I find the right key to sing in?

To know what key to sing in will depend on your vocal range and your song choice. You can try locating the "home note" of the song first. The "home note" is often known as the, "do," or the tonic. Once you have recognised your "do" in the song, you can find out the letter name on a musical instrument or app. Music uses the first seven letters of the English alphabet to identify musical keys. To lower or raise the key of your song, you can move your "do" at a certain interval up or down. Intervals are distances between pitches. For example, "do" to "re," is called a major 2nd, or a whole step. Between "do" and "re" is called a half step, or a minor 2nd. Raise or lower your "do" by whole steps or half steps until you find a suitable key for your vocal range.

The more familiar you are with your vocal range, the easier it will be to find the right keys to sing in. If you don't know your vocal range, I recommend seeking professional help, or asking someone you know who is musically trained. You can test your range by singing the lowest and highest note possible. Use a musical instrument or app to identify the letter name and the octave you're in.

If you are struggling with certain parts of your range, it does not mean you have a "small range." It just means you need to learn how to execute and manage those notes better. Ask yourself, what part of your singing needs adjusting? Is it your breath support? How relaxed is your larynx? Is your singing forced and being pushed from your throat?

Below is a list of voice types for both males and females from the lowest range to the highest.

**MEN**

| | |
|---|---|
| BASSO PROFUNDO | G1 - E4 |
| BASS | E2 - C4 |
| BARITONE | G2 - E4 |
| TENOR | B2 - G4 |
| COUNTERTENOR | F3 - D5 |

**WOMEN**

| | |
|---|---|
| CONTRALTO | F3 - D5 |
| ALTO | G3 - E5 |
| MEZZO SOPRANO | A3 - F5 |
| SOPRANO | C4 - A5 |

## How can I find harmonies?

Harmonies are notes sung simultaneously with the melody. They are often heard in the chorus or bridge of a song. Most common harmonies are third and fifth intervals from the melody, and are often carried by the chords of a song. You can strengthen your ability to hear harmonies with a little ear training. Practice recognising the different intervals used in a song, and try to hear the thirds and fifths from the melody.

# CONCLUSION

As a singer in the last 18 years, I've had the privilege in keeping my singing active through various avenues. I first started singing publicly when I was around 14 years old. You cannot imagine how afraid I was singing in front of people! I was so afraid to the point that nothing would come out! With the encouragement of loved ones, I began to try little by little until I could control my nerves better.

During the earlier years of my singing, I used to struggle with severe vocal strain from bad technique and overuse. I used to hate vocal warm ups because I was always so tired when I did them. The frustration led me to seek for more training. Today, I rarely lose my voice anymore because of what I have learned and developed!

Don't give up or get discouraged if you are not where you want to be right now. Allow yourself to get there in time. Like anything in life, even the things we love will take hard work and discipline. Start with where you are at and build from there. Study, read, seek professional advice and practice, because what you put in is what you will get out.

Try to find opportunities to actively use your singing voice. It could be participating in the school choir, joining the music team at your church, starting a band with some friends, performing at a gig or regularly going for karaoke sessions. You can grow substantially just by performing in front of an audience. If you have stage fright, start with performing in front of the mirror. You can then move on to performing in front of your close family and friends. Overtime, the practice and experience will lead you to greater confidence and control over your voice!

Wishing you all the best,

# MUSIC FROM IVETA

Iveta began writing music in 2002 at the age of 12. After taking up piano lessons, she started to hear all sorts of melodies and lyrics in her head. This began a compilation of songs throughout the course of 16 years before the release of her debut album titled, "Only One," released in 2018.

*"Only One was really a dream come true! I knew that during those long years of writing songs I would one day release my debut album. This project took a little over a year to complete, and in the midst of me getting married and moving over to Singapore! What a crazy ride that was! I am overwhelmed by the faithfulness of God in fulfilling this long-time dream. This album is a love letter to God. It's a testimony of my experience and journey with him for all those years. I've come to find that he really is my only one!" - Iveta*

Visit **harmon-ee-music.business.site** for music and coaching inquires.

# NOTES

# NOTES

# NOTES

# NOTES

# NOTES

# NOTES

# NOTES

# NOTES

# NOTES

# NOTES